POCKETS

THE PROBLEM WITH SOCIETY IS IN WOMEN'S CLOTHING

AUDREY N. GLICKMAN

WORD ASSOCIATION PUBLISHERS
www.wordassociation.com
1.800.827.7903

Printed in the United States of America.

ISBN: 978-1-63385-329-4

Library of Congress Control Number: 2019912706

Published by
Word Association Publishers
205 Fifth Avenue
Tarentum, Pennsylvania 15084

www.wordassociation.com

1.800.827.7903

TABLE OF CONTENTS

Like a sheep in wolf's clothing, the happiness of society is hidden inside women's wear.

It's in the pockets.

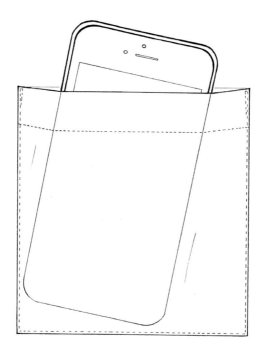

Or rather it's in the **lack** of pockets. No wonder we can't find that happiness!

POCKETS OF DESPAIR

There are not enough pockets for us women, and the ones we have are too small and oddly shaped, and hands do not fit into them.

And this is how half the world is dressed!

We have a pervasive despair: despair *for* a pocket, despair *about* a pocket. We are all despairing, many quietly but some with great vigor. Despairing and desperate, in our pockets of despair. De-spare me, please!

Oh, sure. You think right away of the happy pockets - pockets of joy, pockets of glee, pockets of exuberance. A pocketful of miracles! Well, although I enjoy being cheerful, maybe later. For the moment, the cheery pockets are all hidden by my disgruntledness. You may ultimately agree, and get into my snit and drive off with me. (You may prefer to get into the more compact and fuel-efficient huff. Get into what you wish, there is room on the road.)

What's that? There are more important concerns in this modern world? I put forth the theory that all the world's problems are created, caused, and instigated by pockets.

Pockets can contain so much: cash and change, hankies and watches, joy and trouble, famine and war, invention and discovery... and also those stray ends of a tissue that twist off before you get to use it and fly from the pocket only in polite company.

Seems like everything is affected by pockets.

In this tidy volume, we will explore pockets. Hold on to your hat.

CLOTHING-
MINE
DOESN'T FIT

CHAPTER 1

ECONOMY OF POCKETS

How do we decide what to wear on our bodies each day?

How do *you* decide? By the weather? The time of day, the time of year, the time of month? What your spouse likes? What you like? By where you're going? By your job? By your age?

Does some outside force make your decisions?

Do all your clothes follow the same functionality? Do you go to the department store and ask for a whole bunch of your favorite frilly tops in various colors and a whole bunch of those comfortable straight pants to go with them, and walk away happy?

One of each in every color.

Do you even know what a department store is? Maybe you pore through the internet searching for all the long-sleeved, v-necked, knee-length dresses that don't need belts, in shades of purple, with matching hats and shoes, and when you find them you buy them.

Or maybe you want more variety. Probably most of us are not so self-limiting that we find one thing we like and stick with it. Except for work uniforms, we tend to wear different styles every day. All skirts are not the same, sweaters come in wide variety. Even blue jeans come in hundreds of styles; one person may wear several types, though not all at once.

Let's look more closely at some of our habits.

Take our friend Shifra Lithpo, an accountant. When she peers into her closet in the morning, she's thinking (she told me) about whether she'll see a client that day, whether she'll be walking in the rain, and whether that nice young man from the law firm down the hall might happen to pass by when she's walking to the mailroom with a bunch of tax returns.

Shifra finds something to wear that fits all those potentialities while color-coordinating with tax returns, and she puts it on her body. She finds shoes to match, with the same considerations in mind, and then she is off and running for the day. We could all be just like Shifra, I say!

We could all be just like Shifra

"But wait!" asserts Angelica Moosepierre, tugging on my pocketless jacket. "I'm not Shifra! I don't care about the handsome lawyer down the hall!"

Angie seems a bit frantic.

"What about those days when I plan to run between the raindrops of the predicted thunderstorms, put air into my tires and buy gas, drop off the kid at school, go to the office to face a pile of work, change the toner in the copier, and see two clients, go from the second client to pick up my kid after school to get to his baseball game, sit on the wet grass for the game, stop for dinner with a few of the other kids and their parents, and rush home to walk the dog? How do I dress for that?"

"Washable," I say. "And maybe waterproof. With pockets."

Washable? With *pockets*??!! We've struck a chord – er, someone has struck a chord, and it sounds like an E-minor diminished seventh with vibrato and bass tritone tremolo.

*Angelica tugs on
the author's pocketless jacket.*

No need for chords. Of course I was just teasing! Who has washable clothing that you can wear to the office and see clients, that won't be ruined by sitting on wet grass and has pockets for game snacks, meter money, napkins, doggie poop bags, and a couple hand-wipes? Who besides a man?

Practically the only way to get clothing like this is to make it yourself. They just don't sell it, or if they do it's made for hiking or traveling, it costs a fortune, and it only comes in one color.

The perfect solution would be a chain of stores with walk-in computers that scan our bodies and ask what properties we want in our clothes down to the very minutest detail. Then we would punch in our desired style, fit, and design, and have our clothing produced on demand.

I'll take a pair of high-waisted smooth-fit straight-leg pants with six pockets, each deep enough to hold my phone and comfy enough to hold my keys. And let's have a loose tunic over the pants, with two side pockets hidden in the seams. Add a jacket with pockets, because my office is always cold. And I want all the pieces stretchable for those occasional days of water-weight gain.

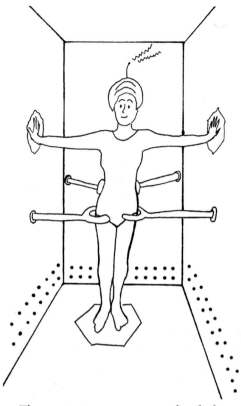

The computer measures us for clothing.

I want that outfit in six colors and patterns, in washable fabrics for each season, at an affordable price.

And the clothing appears, in the proper size and color, with the designated pockets.

Alas, it's not happening. It isn't likely to happen, because the fashion industry is way too big, and those who dictate what we're going to wear have way too much power. And this is, for the moment, an economic impediment.

POCKET ECONOMICS

Economics is a soft science, abounding with theories and predicted outcomes. I put forth that clothing is also soft, maybe with not so many theories but with a lot of predicted outcomes which usually do not live up to the promises in the advertisements.

Of course it will.

Who knows anything about economics? If you do, I invite you to weigh in. I haven't consulted any economists in writing this book, though sometimes I read what they write. (If they contact me, I'll let you know.)

I do know a smattering about finance, just a bit from dabbling in it for a living, serving on a few boards, and – the best economic education – raising children.

Back in junior high school they forced us to take "home economics." So let me don the pocketless apron I made in Home Ec, and say:

> *Today's economy is all*
> *about who has pockets,*
> *where they are,*
> *how big they are,*
> *and what's inside them.*

Where's my spatula? Let me lay it on you, Macduff.

CHAPTER 2

WHO HAS THE POCKETS?

One of my main complaints about pockets is that only those with power have them. By that I mostly mean *men*.

Please don't stop reading! This book is not a screed for or against any particular gender or gender expression. Everyone needs pockets!

I'm talking about the clothing industry and the inordinate effect it has had on our economy.

Men's pockets are enabling them to retain power. And also their keys.

Men's pants with whole hands in pockets.

Women's pants with one key and one tissue in pocket.

We have become a society rife with pocket devices. We carry our devices wherever we go, we work with them, we play with them, we nag ourselves with them, we date through them, we connect by them. They tell us when to be where, and how to get there. We call Mom with them, and it gives Mom yet another way to try to reach us.

We carry them with us from the moment we awake to the moment we go to sleep, and then some.

Yet a Google search for women's office-appropriate workplace garments with pockets large enough to hold an iPhone 5 (let alone an iPhone 10) turned up *only* a nice pair of Carhartt stretch Force Utility pants for $60. Definitely not office wear, at least not where I work, but really good for what they are. (Carhartt has always understood certain things. Would that overalls would be appropriate office wear! That can be our next revolution.)

The informal search also showed a bit of history. In 2014 when the iPhone 6 came out, makers of women's jeans told reporters that they were "considering" larger pockets. There are no reports thereafter that that they ever produced the jeans with larger pockets, and I certainly haven't found any. I did find a blog post by a woman with an insulin pump who wanted a pocket in which to carry it.

How long has it been, Mr. Clothing Manufacturer? Since the days of the Walkman, with its obviously masculine name? Since the days of the transistor radio, which fit neatly into men's shirt pockets?

Your Research & Development Department is a bit behind the times if I can't fit my iPhone 6 into my jeans pocket.

I guess we've digressed from office wear here to jeans! But if I am going out to a park to toss around a frisbee with a friend, why should his cell phone be firmly secured in his larger jeans pocket while mine is sticking out at an odd angle, with 40% of it showing above the top of the pocket, ready to jump out and fall off a cliff?

We are constant ads for Fool-Proof Cases.

THE CURSE OF THE PURSE

Women carry purses. What do we carry in them? Our identification and cards, comb, makeup, cash, change, feminine products, maybe mints, hairspray, and perfume, maybe medication, maybe other things. And our cell phone.

If the purse is large enough, we can carry an umbrella, a pen and paper, a spare diaper, a candy bar, lunch: things men might carry in a brief case or shoulder bag, although we may carry those, too. Sometimes men ask us to carry things for them in our purses, just so their pockets will be lighter!

Men's suits have four to six pockets in the pants, possibly a pocket inside the waistband, one inside the belt, and five or more pockets in the jacket. If there is a vest, that gives them two more pockets. Men could carry the contents of a woman's purse inside their pockets with no effort.

There are now-famous photos of The Honorable Justice Ruth Bader Ginsburg as a younger woman teaching class with her pocketbook just standing there on the desk.

Nowadays, we don't keep our purses on the desk for fear of theft. But we have to keep them handy.

Let's say we're somewhere in our workplace, maybe walking in the hallway from one colleague's office to another's, or maybe between the rest room and our respective rooms or desks. The boss shouts, "Impromptu meeting, my office, now!" (The boss has always been a boor, we live with it.) Women employees must scoot to their offices to retrieve their phones, just in case they need their calendars, note-taking ability, or other information. If they may need their purses, or if the office is not secure, they drag the purses along, too.

The men get all the good spots.

Thus the men always arrive first, needing to do no fetching, unburdened with items in hand, taking the best seats for political maneuvering or for buttering up the boorish boss.

The only thing a man can't carry in his pockets is a cup of coffee. And even that one is a close call.

See the cup of coffee and a donut in this man's jacket pockets.

CHAPTER 4

PROPOSAL

I propose we women simply stop buying any clothing for work that does not have large pockets.

Angie wears her only outfit with pockets to work every day. It is getting threadbare.

Wait! What am I saying? I don't want to limit our revolution! Let's stop buying any clothing *at all* that doesn't have large pockets!

Picketing for pockets.

We need pockets all the time! We need pockets in our evening gowns!

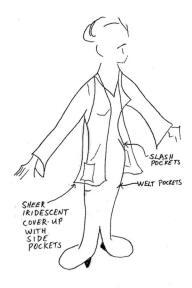

We need pockets in our shorts! Pockets in our dresses! Pockets in our long underwear!

And I don't mean one-inch-deep appliqués that pretend to be pockets but which launch our money and tissues toward the ground every time we sit down. I mean real pockets that can contain *things*.

We need pockets in our sweaters, pockets in our coats. We need pockets in our bathing suits!

And we need pockets even bigger than those that men have!

CHAPTER 5

PROPOSAL RETHOUGHT

Oh, dear. If we stop buying clothing, I guess we may end up going to work in the emperor's new clothes. And we definitely can't put pockets into them!

It is possible that clothing designers have servants carrying around their personal items for them, or maybe the purse designers give the clothing designers a kickback if they omit pockets from their products.

Maybe it costs a lot of money to build in pockets. But it will cost a lot more if we all stop buying clothing *without* them.

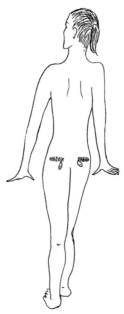

Birthday Suit.

Let's you and I go into business. We shall call the company Purse-less.

CHAPTER 6

STYLE

N ow, then. We ought to broaden our look at women's clothing.

The style issue is a huge debate, but if we just tackle the pockets first, we can move on to further equity, maybe even Washability For All.

So we shall begin with pockets. But just for a moment, before we begin, let's dream a bit bigger. Let's look at the whole person in clothing.

Certainly we rarely see men wearing skin-tight clothing, sheer stockings, or high heels to the office. Do women really have to put forth that look? And if you feel strongly that we should be dressing that way, or even if you simply like it for yourself, do pockets really interfere with the image?

Back in the 1960s and '70s, everyone was wearing skin-tight clothing. Women wore full-coverage bras under see-through blouses, and men wore their shirts open halfway down the front. Our jeans came all the way up to our lower hip-bones, both men and women. Shorts were short for all genders. Everyone could see most of what we had.

The 1960s, historians are still trying to explain it all.

Then we survived the polyester era, which was bad for all of us. Back then, sometimes even men's clothing did not have pockets, though patch pockets on a man's powder-blue polyester double-knit leisure suit might have put it over the top.

The author's little brother in a suit in 1975.

Nowadays the genders are more differentiated. For instance, men are wearing baggier pants, and men's shorts fall way down past their knees. Er, many men have their shorts falling down, but what I mean is the bottom of the shorts rests below the men's knees. Women, meanwhile, are wearing what we used to term "hot pants" for shorts.

To work, men wear business casual shirts with sweaters while women wear skin-tight suits with pencil skirts (no pockets) and décolleté skin-tight waist-cinching suit jackets with only a camisole underneath.

So let's look deeper at women's wear, for something besides pockets seems to have gone awry.

Looking deeper, we find underwear! In the bra department we absolutely need to revert to the 1970s, or even the 1950s. In the '50s one could buy a constructed bra (usually in cone shapes) made of woven cotton stitched in concentric rings, with adjustable elastic straps and no plastic wires inside. Being cotton, it breathed, and it felt healthy. It held up under sweaters as well as under lightweight blouses and crop tops. And if you fell asleep in it, it didn't leave a dent in your rib cage.

In the mid-1970s, we went lightweight, minimalist. Just enough to cover and to hold things up. Good under a see-through blouse and good with a heavy sweater, too.

But now! How the boobs have fallen.

In 2017 I went to a certain Undergarment Store, from which I had bought bras since the 1980s. My old Elizabeth style bras were finally biting the dust, I could no longer take tucks in the stretched-out elastic, and I needed to replace them. Being average, I wear a 34B. It's a very common size. I've had children, and although it has occurred to me to hire a handsome fellow to walk around behind me holding up my breasts, it is much more practical just to buy some good new underwear.

The woman at the underwear store told me authoritatively that nowadays women no longer wear the size that they measure. She brought in a dozen different models for me to try, and she sold me three bras in two different styles, two different colors, in size 32D. She told me I would get used to them,

I would love them. The $150 they cost was a lesson well learned.

Wearing those bras is like wearing armor.

Armor plated bra

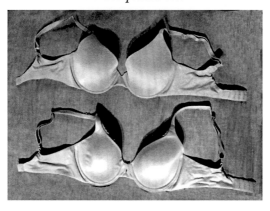

Actual bra types purchased

The wires under the more-than-full-coverage half-inch-thick padding stab me in my underarms all day. I can't carry things at work without feeling as if my chest has come loose and is battling with whatever I'm carrying. My boobs are floating and swimming around inside the bra like guppies in a bowl. I hate those bras.

Yet I cannot find any bra anywhere that does the job as I define it! The new ones everywhere are just awful. And they do not need to be, because the same companies used to make better choices.

As I have mentioned to store clerks, I just want to be held up, I don't need to be blossomed forth.

I do realize we have digressed from pockets, which is still the topic of this book.

But then again, it would be very efficient if a great bra were made with a pocket in the middle, ready to hold whatever one needs. Great place to store money, tissues, feminine supplies. Designers? Get on it! And by the way, get rid of those stretchy straps – no one wants everything to start sagging halfway through the day, we want things held firmly!

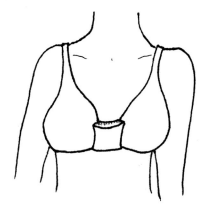

A bra with a pocket

There! With pockets incorporated we can order up a new bra or two from our clothing-making machine and include it in our package.

GETTING BACK TO STYLE

Maybe we should begin by changing style a little bit at a time. For the moment, let's get back to pockets and consider the portable phone. Phones stay with us all the time, they have heftier size than their immediate predecessors, they have to be instantly retrievable, and they also may have radiation issues.

So let's build a standard pocket away from our body core – especially important for pregnant women – and incorporate it into all our clothing.

ENGINEERING DETAILS

Here's a good place for a pocket, right along the thigh. The pocket can be supported on the side seam, or suspended from the waistband, built with a slim smooth welt, made to support a phone. The same pocket on the other side could carry feminine items, an insulin pump, a wallet, or all of these items. The cell phone would be far enough from the body core for safety of our internal organs, and of any children we may be gestating.

Of course, deep enough standard side-front pockets could serve a similar function.

There is no reason pockets are currently made just one inch deep, except for the manufacturers to save money and keep women subjugated.

Even Shifra Lithpo, who by the way now has had two dates with that young attorney down the hall, would be eager for a pocket to carry the security key she needs in her office.

When a designer creates a women's suit jacket with a peplum, why not put a pocket into the top of the peplum? Or into the side seam of the peplum? Or into the underside of the peplum? Why not make the whole peplum a pocket? Why not put a pocket into the pencil skirt where it would be hidden under the peplum?

Angelica Moosepierre with a side pocket.

And by the way, after we have passed age 40, or age 50, even though we may still be slim, not all of us want to wear pencil skirts with peplum jackets. The Flower Children and Baby Boomers and Suburban Housewives all have reached a "certain age" and may not want to dress like a bunch of chickie-doos and tchatchkies.

Shifra Lithpo's grandmother, seen here, needs some pockets. She also needs a different style of suit.

You know, the Flappers of the 1920s had hip flasks strapped to their thighs to hold their prohibited booze. Talk about a great pocket!

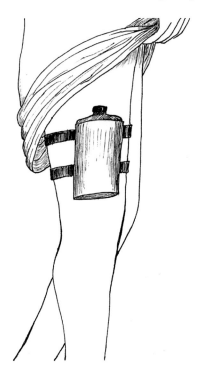

CHAPTER 7

MAKING MORE POCKETS

We could even have more pockets than just the standard! When I build clothing, I build pockets inside pockets. If I'll need parking quarters, I put them into a pocket built along the inside wall of my main front pants pocket, so that the change doesn't jingle when I walk. I can put any needed medication in the same sort of inside pocket. If someone should suddenly hand me an ice cream sundae, I will need lactase tablets, so I carry those in one of the inside pockets in my jackets, and I've made a little pouch for them (a floating pocket), too. One should never have to turn down an ice cream sundae for lack of pockets.

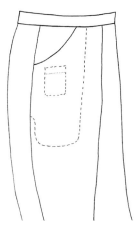

Pants pocket with a pocket inside.

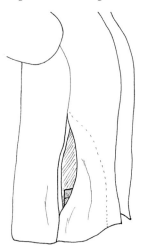

Jacket pocket with a pocket inside.

An ice cream sundae.

I've built suit jackets with double pockets, too. If the main pocket is deep enough – even if it is sewn into a vertical seam – it can have a secondary pocket inside.

And why should men be the only ones with pockets in the inside of their suit jackets? I've sewn inside pockets into pocket-less jackets just to hold my cell phone. I have sewn them into sweaters, too.

(I know, I am weak and find it difficult to resist buying a jacket or a sweater I like just because it doesn't have a pocket, especially if it is on sale. So much for our movement.)

Sometimes I rip open the seams of jackets to insert pockets. But we shouldn't have to do that! It's time-consuming and negates the very reason we buy ready-made clothing.

My son has a pair of pants with a tiny pocket just under the waist in the back, which would be big enough to hold identification and credit cards.

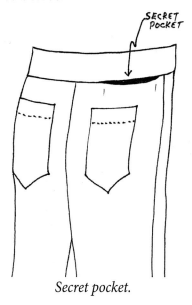

Secret pocket.

I want one of those, too!

CHAPTER 8

MORE THAN JUST POCKETS

O f course we must wear more than just pockets. The rest of our clothing has issues, too, some of which I mentioned earlier. Those matters can be part of our second revolution.

I know that some women love their clothing. We can learn to love anew.

Let's spend a moment on shoes, for instance.

Loving a gnu.

Loving a shoe.

Why are women still wearing high heels?

Who tells us that our legs look better in them, and why do we believe them? I live in a hilly neighborhood, and my calves look just great without heels.

Of course I wore them when I was younger – I was an expert at navigating the cobblestone streets with streetcar tracks in Downtown Pittsburgh in my gold-and-yellow stiletto heels without twisting an ankle. But my feet were never happy about it.

In fact, when shoe makers make heels the same height for all sizes of their shoe models, they do a vast disservice to those of us with Size 5 feet. Four-inch heels spread over a Size 10 foot can be much more manageable. And at least put a pocket in that wedgie espadrille!

Some women think the sound of their high heels click-clacking on the school or office floor conveys an aura of power, but my second-grade teacher click-clacked all day with an air of haughtiness and we all disliked her then and have little good to say to this day. To us the sound represented her exerting elephantine authority, approaching our classroom to dole out torture, rather than imparting knowledge.

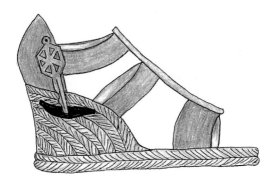

Pocket Wedgie Espadrille.

Get past it, women; you can be powerful in flats as well.

Wall sign:

The power is not in your insteps. It is in your pockets.

Many power-seekers also think that if their breasts are high and their waist is slim and they wear a lot of makeup, they have influence. Are men doing similar primping and fretting and fussing? Are they wearing push-up t-shirts and tushy-squeezing undies to work? Okay, maybe a few are. Are they padding their pants or wearing codpieces in the office? Are their shoes baring half their foot in the name of style, despite below-zero temperatures outside, as we know some women do?

This man is really primped up.

So why are women doing these things? When we are at work, most of us are not fishing for a romance. I wish Shifra Lithpo a pocketful of success, but I think my clothing should reflect my personality, make my personage look capable and comfortable and hard-working, and should otherwise leave everything else to the imagination. I'm not known for drab clothing, but the bra from the Undergarment Store has always been hidden far underneath during the workday.

And back to those shoes for a moment! Heels or not, we want our shoes and boots waterproof! Why are we supposed to be willing to spend $200+ on a pair of delicate suede shoes that will get water-stained in the first rain?

Why do boot makers create winter wear that cannot stand up to snow? And why do they add high heels so that we must work harder to walk on the ice?

Forsooth! Floods and hurricanes are proliferating! Monsoons are flying, icebergs are melting, land is sliding! Bitter blizzards are booming!

And when our feet get wet we might catch cold.

Overall, we women do have the benefit of a variety of shapes of clothing being acceptable, and we could expand that variety. We don't need to become like men in suits, who express their individuality only with neckties. (Men don't need to be that limited, either!) We should seek practicality, and settle for no less.

Clothing makers, are you out there? Please, oblige us! Designers, it's not about body decoration, it is about daily life and making our way in the world.

Maybe this is all part of our third, fourth, and fifth revolutions. At least we are defining our goals.

The bottom line is that we want all of these pocket-packed items of clothing to be just as inexpensive or costly, and as varied and expressive, as the clothing we are already buying and wearing. If you're a person who readily spends $400 at Ferdstrom's for a suit to wear to work, you ought to get pockets in it. If you buy items on sale at Stone Mart or QMart or Happy Mart, you ought to get pockets in them as well, useable pockets, with ample room.

Washable Pocketed Clothing.

We will talk later about whether all clothing is machine-wash, tumble-dry. Why wouldn't it be? We'll remember to empty the pockets first.

GLOBAL
POCKETS

CHAPTER 1

HOW BIG ARE THE POCKETS?

A lthough pockets could solve many of our problems, I'm not really blaming our pocket-less clothing for the current state of the world, nor even for the plight of women.

I am just observing the obvious.

Those who have big pockets like to keep them full, which leads us to that squirming morass of predatory worms: the wealthy and powerful. I'd like to go deep for a bit.

I think that politics is the hapless victim of a larger economic war.

Regardless our political holdings, it is obvious that money has become more and more unfairly distributed, everywhere.

Looking only at the United States, we see that the wealthy are very, very wealthy. And we have over the years given them some freedom from taxes that we have not afforded to the less wealthy. What's that you say, gentleman in the smoking jacket reading over your wife's shoulder? Those of us who earn less get away with paying less? Yes, it is proportional, kind sir. I pay over one-third of my salary in taxes while you are paying one-twelfth of your salary. And the dollar amounts are likely the same.

So, based on wealthy folks paying less in taxes, the country is ever more in debt. And from whom do we borrow? We borrow from those wealthy! Yes, the same wealthy persons to whom we have given tax breaks are now lending us money. Therefore, as we pay them interest on their loans, they will be needing ever bigger pockets as they profit from their tax reduction.

In order to keep those wealthy getting wealthier, they finance the campaigns of the politicians who will support their interests, and it becomes a vicious cycle of hands in pockets.

And how about the politicians themselves? We are seeing more and more women involved in government, but oftentimes without pockets.

Maybe that's a good thing, in terms of the wealthy not wanting to bother with a politician who has no pockets. But more likely that lack of pockets bears witness to why we still see political cartoons using the same tired female stereotypes about not paying for dinner and probably using botox. Give those women pockets! Even in the political cartoons.

Meanwhile, can the rest of us get wealthy? What will it take?

DO YOU WORK FULL TIME?

Do you work for pay? Do you work full time? What *is* "full time"?

There's a threshold at which you decide whether your work is part-time, full-time or all the time, whether it's something that you do during a part of the day, during only the part of the day you consider to be the "work day," or virtually all of your life. You decide whether your work will be gainful employment or without financial compensation.

What are your boundaries? How do you judge whether you work "full time"?

What are your goals? Does the doctor treating cancer patients have the same goals as an investment banker? Does a bus driver have the same goals as a preschool teacher? Does a computer scientist have the same goals as a sociologist?

And how do you do your business? Does it merge into your personal life? Do you do business on your personal electronics even though you are not self-employed? Do your clients have your personal cell number, even if you work for someone else?

What are you thinking, say, when you don't care about the consequences to the office in accepting a spur-of-the-moment invitation to spend the day on the beach rather than show up at work?

Does your employer limit your work to 35½ hours a week to avoid paying full-time salary and benefits? Do you care so much about your work and your clients and your business that you spend every moment - except *maybe* dinnertime - working?

Do you have a spouse? Children? An extended family?

Maybe you define your work by a salary threshold, maybe by a trust threshold. Some professions carry more trust, and maybe less pay, such as minister, parking enforcement officer, short-order cook.

If you're a judge, for instance, and you're paid $25,000 a year, you still have to comport yourself as a judge 24/7. Sometimes you have to work more than 40 hours a week, without overtime pay. Maybe you resent it, maybe you don't even notice the disparity.

This is true for many professions, from middle management up, and sometimes from there down as well.

Let's pause for a tribute to one of my favorite coworkers of all time, Ruthie. Ruthie was a messenger in a law firm, for decades, and she was the stuff of legend. She was loyal as anyone, and was ready for any internal or external messengering that might be required. The tale describes her bringing a package she had fetched back to the office, when a driver failed to see her legally crossing at the crosswalk, and hit her. The ambulance came, and Ruthie flatly refused to be taken to the hospital until someone promised to get her package up to the attorney waiting for it. Messengering was her business and she was committed to it. The firm took care of her when arthritis began to get the better of her, and they defined her job to include only internal work, delivering mail and copy jobs, and making certain there was always a pot of coffee going anywhere in the offices. The loyalty went both ways.

Ruthie

That was a long time ago, though, and one wonders whether this sort of two-way loyalty might still be found and fostered. More often we see the opposite.

Sometimes organizations will define a certain position as "exempt," meaning the employee can't put in for overtime, even when the person in the position should be paid on an hourly basis and qualify for overtime. Then the employee is given an inordinate amount of work with no assistance, such that it takes longer than the hours allotted. Needing the paycheck, the employee does whatever it takes. (Such employees usually don't need very big pockets for cashing their paychecks.)

With the recent slump in the power of labor unions, and the rise of non-traditional jobs in the tech and medical fields, we are seeing more and more of this injustice. The employee must be available all day, every day, must use his/her own computer and phone as a contact for work, is given bogus perks such use of a treadmill down the hall with no time ever to use it, and often is scheduled right through lunch hour.

We also are seeing a decline in traditional support employees, and an expectation by the employer that the "exempt" employees will support themselves. These employees do their own document and presentation preparations, compose and send and receive their own correspondence, make and receive phone calls, schedule their own appointments, do their own filing, and make their own travel arrangements. They must know how to type, spell, compose and send correspondence, use correct grammar and business form, make and receive phone calls, and juggle a schedule, in addition to knowing the business in which they are employed. And they do this all from their own home. Perhaps they need no pockets in their homes, but they have to be presentable for video conference calls.

Having served as support staff at various levels of business and government, I know that support burden is huge. With busy middle-to-upper management, there should be at least one support person to every couple managers, to free up the manager to actually do the business of the company and still have time to live a life.

Home Office – With Nightstand Pockets

Thus we have a generation of young persons desperately trying to pay off college loans, working 24 hours a day, tethered to their devices, some working from home, essentially supplying the company's machinery, office space, and supplies as well as on-call personnel.

And they know no different: they profess to being happy!

This younger generation doesn't keep the formalities of past business persons. Unless they are lawyers, they likely keep very few paper files. They may not wear formal clothing to an office, or if they do it isn't a tie and jacket for men with sock garters and waistcoat with watch fob. Women don't generally dress formally anymore, either, although if they do they may wear those pencil skirts and peplum jackets (without pockets, of course, as described earlier), and those $400 high heels that would melt in the rain.

These young folks begin their business correspondence not with "Dear Dr. Hossenpfeffer:" but with "Hi, Armand," thus further blurring the line between home and work. They don't know how to post a letter, don't know what a stamp is. If someone needs something tomorrow, they go to the same box store to which they go for large numbers of photocopies, and have it sent.

Let's meet young Arabelle Lithpo (Shifra's cousin), who wrote that "Hi, Armand" at the beginning of her business letter. Arabelle, who works for a public relations firm which targets the medical profession on behalf of its clients, deals with large conglomerates and thus speaks with doctors all over the world. Because what sells in Bali may not sell in Baltimore, and vice-versa, she must speak with doctors everywhere differently.

And Arabelle must travel to them, with only a carry-on bag – which bags are getting smaller and smaller – and a purse and no pockets. I have not asked the doctors what they think about reading "Hi, Armand" and seeing a person traveling without pockets. Perhaps one of you readers is a doctor and could advise me.

However, I predict that these young persons will be burned out within twenty years, if not ten. Their pockets, if any, will be just as empty as when they started their jobs. And their hard playing – squeezed in at the last minute when they find they have an evening off – will become just as old, as will their speed-scanning of a good book now and then, or their thinking once a year about maybe creating a family but postponing it.

MORE FULL TIME?

Who else works full time?

We pay professional football players millions of dollars a year, so I guess they are working full time.

(Personally, I've never understood the difference between a salary of $13 million and a salary of $12 million. What qualifies a football player for that extra million? What on earth does he do with it? Possibly there will be large healthcare bills later on, but the $12 million should suffice. And why then do the football franchises expect to tap our tax dollars for an extra million to build additions on stadiums when salaries are so high? **And more to the point, as long as we are asking, do football players have pockets in those uniforms?**)

The heads of major corporations now make far more, relatively, than their underlings, percentage-wise, than they have since the days of the Rockefellers and Vanderbilts, or possibly ever. Why do we permit that? And then why do we give extra tax shelters to those wealthy folks, and to the corporations as well? And we buy their products, and get them wealthier. And we let our mutual funds invest in them, in hopes of ever being able to retire.

I won't even discuss the extra freedoms we afford the corporations such as freedom to pollute, use of eminent domain, and freedom to base the corporation in a particular state or in another country to optimize (minimize) or avoid taxes. Not to mention giving freedom to act as a "person" in ways other than just for signing a contract (that was the original intent for corporate personhood), along with freedom to influence our elections, and freedom to lie to us in commercials and in other ways.

Right now, a third of my salary is withheld for taxes. I also pay real estate taxes, sales taxes, utility taxes, driving privilege assessments, dog licenses, and various other public contributions.

Do our wealthy pay the same percentage? Do the top 1% of wealth holders, the very wealthy, pay the same percentage? And are they just as worried about how they will send their children to college, make major home repairs, or ever retire?

How many millions of dollars are enough per year for any individual?

How big are their virtual pockets, anyway?

CHAPTER 2

HOW SMALL ARE YOUR POCKETS?

L et's get back to the basic practicality of pockets, regardless whether we have enough money to put into them.

Take a survey of your clothing, please. If you are female and you count each pocket large enough for a cell phone per article of clothing, and average such a pocket in more than 50% of your clothing, you are doing quite well. The average of our averages, though, is less than optimal.

I do believe that if women's clothing had sufficient pocketage – to coin a new term – we would have more control of our lives and the world.

As we discussed before, I understand that some women want to wear form-fitting clothing. Men used to do that, too, when I was younger, not to mention what they wore back in the 1400s with jerkins and codpieces and such. But I find the motivation sometimes to be troubling.

Wearing skin-tight clothing on a date, or in a rhumba contest, or to karaoke night might be okay. Why wear it to work, unless the date is immediately thereafter?

And if it is the case that many women want to wear skin-tight clothing, let's find a way to insert pockets somewhere.

I've been building my own pockets since I was a teenager. I began making my own clothing when I was 11 years old because I couldn't find any bell-bottom pants in my size. The patterns back then often did not include pockets, and I had to learn how to make them.

Over the years, though I have decreased production of bell-bottoms, I have increased making pocketage, and have devised many types of pocket for various styles of clothing.

For instance, many times I've bought simple skirts or pants and opened the side seams and inserted pieces of lining material or muslin cut into this shape:

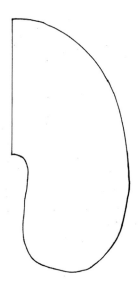

One must make certain that the top part –
the vertical straight side – is large enough
for you to comfortably insert your hand, and
also has room for seams around the outside.

Sometimes when making pockets of this
type or any other type for bottom clothing,
where the pocket will ride along the thigh,
I add a second pocket inside the first, thus:

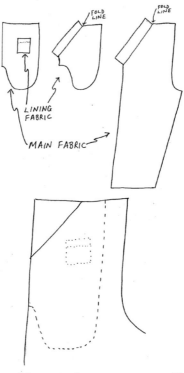

Even making a jacket, sometimes I'll insert a secondary pocket along the body side of the larger pocket. These secondary pockets are good for parking change, for an aspirin, cough drop, or necessary pills or a pill box. (As I mentioned in Chapter 7, I use them for Milk Digestant Tablets, so that I can always be ready to eat a slice of pizza or an ice cream sundae should someone hand it to me.)

Also as I mentioned earlier, sometimes I fall in love with a blazer, washable and on sale, but with no pockets. How can I resist? So I take it home and cut open the darts or the princess seams and insert pockets.

My latest creation is a supported side pocket for pants. I build a welted pocket into the outsides of the thighs of pants, and support it with seam-binding tape or extra-wide seam allowances so that it is suspended on the sides from the waistband. Thus it can hold either my phone or my wallet, down away from my body core. This is even possible in flimsy fabric, as long as it is properly suspended, or attached to the lining.

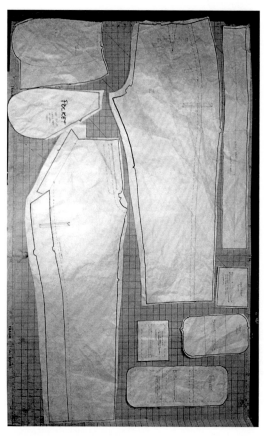

Prototype pattern for pants with side pocket.

I thought about patenting that last pocket, but I'd rather see the whole world have them, than to make money on the design and have to produce them myself.

Of course, it is relatively easy to make a rectangle of fabric, finish the edges, and attach it to the lining of a jacket. One need only dream the pocket, and then make it.

HOWEVER, one also needs the time to do this. And as we keep saying, we no longer have so much expendable time.

If the clothing companies would offer as many pocket styles as they do jeans styles, we would have a booming market. And by "styles" I don't mean whether the pocket has colored stitching holding it, or rhinestones on it, or a little zipper beside it. I mean real pockets of varied sizes and locations and uses. Surprise us! The most inventive pockets get our money.

CHAPTER 3

BACKPACKS WITH POCKETS

O ur pockets get picked by the higher educational system.

A COLLEGE EDUCATION

In the 1970s, Lil Beldengreen attended a state-affiliated university, and paid $512 per term for three terms a year (in-state, not including room and board). When she graduated, after various short-term employment, she got a full-time entry-level job in a somewhat related field with an $8,000/year salary, a training program, healthcare plan, and a chance for promotion. Many of her "bosses" (she supported twelve persons and managed 18 phone lines) had been through the company training program, having worked in other professions before starting at the bottom. Former teachers seemed to be prominent among them.

Backpacks often have a lot of pockets, and many women do use backpacks rather than purses.

The tuition at that same university now is $9,540 per term. Therefore, the starting, entry-level salary with a training program, healthcare, and a chance for promotion (if it even existed anymore) should pay $149,062.50 a year.

In truth, now there are precious few jobs with training programs and a chance of promotion, let alone healthcare. In fact, that training program ended at Lil's work just when she was ready to be promoted. They began having in college interns who were majoring in what the company did for a living and were free labor, who then became available for hire.

Meanwhile, college tuition has gotten completely out of hand, although there is little evidence that the lowest levels of the teaching staff – even professors – are seeing any of the money. There are more administrators, the learning spaces are refurbished much more often to keep up with technology, and there is building sprawl.

Wherever the money is going, we are permitting it to go there. It is going into *someone's* pockets.

Nowadays, the students must decide early on – even in middle school – what they want to study, because the employers will be looking for individuals with a narrow set of specific skills and knowledge, maybe with prior internships, and will not accept anyone else.

And then many students learn that given all the required courses and prerequisites and the conflicting times at which they are offered, it will take them five or six years to graduate.

It isn't hard to see the waste in this system. Students at many schools don't learn enough about the world in general, about other fields, about other people, to make them well-rounded individuals (except possibly those who have taken up sociology and spend time studying the rest of us). Certainly they don't study business correspondence and other amenities of the working world. And once they graduate, they can only hope that the narrow fields they have chosen remain viable economically.

NO COLLEGE EDUCATION

There are many professions that do not "require" a college education. We learn skills and develop talents for these jobs in other ways, in other places.

I don't know any auto mechanics who studied their professions in college. I do know a few who have a college education, and that is a very good thing overall, as good colleges teach about people and science and technology, train us to think analytically, and open our eyes to others' opinions and expressions and interests, not to mention where the future of the automotive industry may lie.

Those who wait tables are in a similar situation. They may have studied something else. Or they majored in business or hospitality and own the restaurant. And those who sell furniture, bedding, clothing, etc., likely studied something else, too, maybe art or interior design.

Are there many salespersons who majored in marketing? Doesn't seem so to me. If the person selling us a car, or a newspaper, or chewing gum attended college, it was likely for something else.

Those selling us sandwiches or musical instruments may have majored in cooking or music. But the selling part of the job was learned somewhere else.

Plumbers and carpenters and electricians, too, learn somewhere else. And many of them figure out the business end on their own. (Even doctors and pharmacists often have to figure out the business end of things on their own! Even though they attended college.)

Building managers often learn their trades working maintenance with others. Some begin learning by putting themselves through college for something else.

These are the self-starters among us. They know how to deal with people, and how to make us want what they are selling. They also know how to provide what we want.

And these are the folks who struggle to earn a steady living, keep their children in clothing and send them to college, take a vacation now and again, and plan for retirement. We have made economic life for these folks consistently difficult, even though they may not begin adult life with college debt.

BEFORE COLLEGE

Adie Moosepierre, Angelica's sister-in-law, has a millennial son Julius who just after he was born in the late 1980s was given an investment intended for his education. Adie's uncle Sam put in more money for each birthday, on the presumption it would grow and be enough to cover Julius' education. (Had the economy not suffered major downturns while the lad was in college, it would have taken him through all five years.) However, the account was created before anyone had invented a tax-exempt education account, and by the time they had devised such a thing, the account held too much to be converted into an education IRA. Thus young Julius fell into a doughnut hole, and the Moosepierres were forced to pay taxes on the dividends and capital gains through the years. By the time he was a young teenager, the kid was filing his own tax return.

The iniquity wasn't lost on Julius Moosepierre. He wasn't old enough to vote, but had to pay taxes: taxation without representation. He was indignant.

Would, though, that we all had an uncle Sam to pay for our education.

EQUAL OPPORTUNITY BEFORE AND DURING COLLEGE

Yes, there are many economic theories, and maybe mine is more out-of-pocket than you will be comfortable with, but I think we should all be given the same start in life, the same educational boost, regardless our strengths and goals and abilities.

We all proudly seek to have equal rights and to have an equal say in our government, so I think we should all be educated to the best of our ability to learn, and toward the strengths that each of us has. And we should learn about *each other* as well.

The idea that some are *more* equal has long bothered me, especially when we are discussing education. Everyone can learn, and everyone deserves the chance to do so.

Within and beyond education, we are back to discussing whether our pockets are full or empty, are solid and numerous, or are few, sporting holes and moths.

CHAPTER 4

WHY ARE THEIR POCKETS SO FULL?

The pockets of the 99% generally are emptier and the pockets of the wealthy are fuller because we are accepting the way they do business.

They can afford to have their pockets built in.

GENERAL LIVING EXPENSES

Remember we mentioned the days when Lil Beldengreen earned $8,000/year? Back then, she paid $26 per month for a landline phone, $210 per month for apartment rent, and upkeep and insurance on her $250 ten-year-old used car (her good friends the Pomrenkes helped immensely with the initial repair and maintenance, and taught Lil to do work herself to some extent, she should have been louder with her gratitude). At that time, a bus pass to work cost about $35 a month for unlimited rides. And any money Lil put into the bank earned between 9% and 13% interest back in those days.

Eventually Lil saved enough to buy a house. Back then, though, few banks would give a mortgage to a single woman, so she could not actually buy one. But once she was engaged to be married they permitted her to spend her money.

Now the times are different. First of all, women can get mortgages on their own, thank goodness and persistence.

But the expenses we incur have skyrocketed. We are paying for our television, our internet, our individual phone lines, and our devices to manage those commodities. Our car insurance costs an exorbitant amount, many of us pay for our own health insurance (often about half our take-home pay or more), apartments cost more than mortgages used to cost and we pay for each utility as well, and taxes have gone up. Low- to mid-level cars now cost at least four times what fancy cars cost back then. We don't buy record albums and own them forever, we pay monthly fees for listening to music that can be taken away if we don't pay.

Meanwhile, any money we put into the bank earns 0.025% interest. But they charge us 20% to borrow money.

CAPITAL INVESTMENTS

We all make capital investments. We buy $30,000 cars, we buy $1,000 phones, we spend $2,000 on a new washer and dryer. A dishwasher can cost $400 to $1,000 or more. A new stove can cost between $500 and $2,000 or more. A new toilet is a couple hundred dollars and won't match the rest of your bathroom.

These items used to be good investments, because they would last 40 or 50 years. But no longer, because someone has "improved" them all.

This "improvement" is really just a bamboozling of the public.

Lil Beldengreen has a washing machine that recently failed because the electronic door lock sensor, which has its own control board, failed to communicate with the main computer board, causing them both to stop working. The door was shut, but it gave the code for a failed door lock and simply would not wash the clothes.

$450 later, after waiting six weeks, if Lil unplugs it between loads, the ten-year-old washer is working again. Lil prefers this, because her washer does more than the new $1,200 models do, and the new ones have more parts to break. Essentially, though, the machine accomplishes the same thing as the 1970s models did without computers. It washes either rough or gently, with cold, warm, or hot water, and can soak things and rinse extra times.

Does Lil really need the machine to sense a drop of water in her red sock and therefore keep spinning for an extra ten minutes? Does she need it to sense when she has closed the door, or would she rather accept a floor filled with water when she hadn't, so she wouldn't have to endure the failed door lock?

The machines cost ten times as much as in the 1970s, but Lil certainly is not earning ten times as much. And they also now last 1/8 as long, and keep getting more expensive with more complex devices that can malfunction, and we have to pay to have them repaired or replaced. Lil's dad used to know how to fix these things, but now that they have computer boards in them, he has given up.

Even toilets have been "improved." Lil's neighbor, J'Kay Ramblattner, has a toilet. Her toilet got the treatment by a plumber over a decade ago (under J'Kay's husband's watch; J'Kay says he didn't object enough). The plumber replaced the float ball with some sort of standing plastic thing that breaks and leaks and sprays and miscalculates and needs to be replaced about every five years for no reason. Toilets are now dumbed-down, and it's harder to get parts for the older high-end models. The expectation is that we will put a new white toilet into our blue bathroom with the blue tub and blue sink and will replace the toilet every ten years when all the moving parts break, or spend $60 or more every few years having it repaired.

Who is making all that money? And is this really a good economic model? The porcelain part of the fixture has withstood the test of time, so to make more money the companies have fitted the main body with flimsy innards.

J'Kay likens it to her car. "Do I really need my car to have more electronic items to break, when those devices still don't tell me anything further than 'maintenance required'?" she asks.

Everything costs so much more for no good reason.

And then beyond that we give up our security with these new-fangled devices! The Internet of Things? Do we really need garage door openers – which used to last about 60 years but now last only ten – that connect by wi-fi? It takes the machine three seconds longer to start opening the door, wants me to use my cell phone to control it, and risks telling remote spies when I am home or away.

Thermostats and alarm systems and refrigerators and any other device that connects to the Internet are security hazards, and I am against them because we cannot keep them safe. And they often talk with our cell phone, which may hold our financial and medical data, and which connects with our Social Security Number which we permit the phone company to require before they will open an account for us to have the phone. (Don't get J'Kay started about giving our Social Security Numbers to the phone companies! Her Congressman's aide told her he feels it is perfectly okay, and at the end of a 45-minute conversation she had not yet convinced him that having the phone company employee able to look at a list of everyone's "Last Four Social" is not okay.)

Lil Beldengreen's first house had a thermostat that ran on electricity generated by the gas furnace. Old model thermostats used a double-strip of metal which would bend based on the current temperature affecting one metal different from the other. Now Lil's thermostat needs a battery, thus risking freezing the house when they are away and the battery dies.

Everyone has these stories. Again, these "improvements" only mean that the companies can charge more for their products, which more often are made somewhere outside the country, and the devices will be broken within a decade and thus the capital investment will be amortized over a much shorter time. In fact, I would call the purchase of any of these devices an "expense" rather than a "capital investment."

Meanwhile, the folks who run those device manufacturing companies are stuffing their pockets, and the planned obsolescence reflects well on their projections.

The only capital investment we have left is house and real estate. And if we can't keep up with the taxes, we can lose that as well, as anyone whose neighborhood has been subject to gentrification will tell you.

CHAPTER 5

BANKS

U sed to be that a bank was a bank, a checking account was different from a savings account, and those were different from all the other sorts of investments.

Then everything merged together, credit card companies started owning everything, and every banking company became a credit card company. Even if it were possible to save money in the traditional way, it is no longer worth it, as the account earns virtually no interest, or is more risky and thus subject to downturns.

We do have a greater ability now to buy stock in companies that we like, and to monitor the stocks the way we did in social studies class back in high school, and that is a good thing. And we have easy access to the filings companies make with the Securities and Exchange Commission.

But with the decimation of the Glass-Steagall Act (partially of 1932 and of 1933, depending on which form of the legislation we are discussing), the lines between banking and investing have blurred, and all the risk is borne by the investor.

Banks are still making money investing our money, but they are not sharing that interest with us. They used to reinvest in our communities. That fellow borrowing from the bank to build a house or a business was using the money that *we* put into the bank, and his interest payment was paying both the bank and us. (Every year I watch *It's a Wonderful Life* just to reaffirm that that used to be so.)

For the most part, this is no longer the case. (There are a few exceptions, such as mutual banks and credit unions.) Mostly now banks will underwrite a charitable endeavor, such as a race or parade, and call that reinvesting in the community.

Our neighborhood banks have been merged out of existence into larger and larger entities, which give less service and less value. They make money on us using our bank access cards as debit cards (something I am loathe to do, just as I do not wish to bank on line), they get rich on the fees they charge us for various things, and by charging us for what used to be free or used to pay us interest.

The banks that gave us our mortgages to buy houses or loans to start businesses have sold those instruments to bigger and bigger corporations with different rules on our paying them off, different ways of paying our taxes, and a decided lack of grace during tough times such as bad weather events.

Yet, as we mentioned before, at least now women are permitted to buy houses by themselves. With or without pocket doors in the dining room.

CHAPTER 6

ARE POCKETS GENERATIONAL?

If pockets were designed to hold money, it's no wonder the Common Woman has trouble finding clothing containing any.

But what of the different generations? Lil Beldengreen's daughter fully expects to have her cellphone's capabilities simply implanted in her arm one day soon, and figures she won't need to carry it. She still will need pockets, of course, but maybe not for the phone.

(How will we recharge the thing once it is embedded? Will we plug our arms into a terminal overnight? Will we sit on top of an induction charger? And what of those with pacemakers?)

The generational questions are numerous. Younger baby boomers who are only now reaching retirement age waited longer to have their children, and now are finding themselves split between carrying their elderly parents' pills in their purses and carrying their kids' wallets during baseball practice, not to mention whatever the husband asked them to carry.

Lil is split between generations.

Meanwhile, older millennials are also waiting to have children. They may soon find that their own parents need their care and attention when the millennials are a bit younger, because the boomer parents were older when they bore the millennials, but soon enough they will also have young children to tend. And also the boomers are likely to live even longer than their own parents did.

Seems to me we should design the economy around this sort of life-change. Rather than running our economy on making more and more money, we should run it on the betterment of the society as a whole.

One day Shifra Lithpo may have to stop working for a while to take care of her parents, or may need to take time away from work to get them to where they need to go. In fact, we have not yet learned how to design the employment system around caring for children, much less for parents.

And many of the places folks have to be taken – to the dentist, the gerontologist, the orthodontist, daycare (both kids and parents), the Little League game (both kids and parents) – mostly require transport during work hours. It is very similar to needing to be home or at the parents' home for deliverers, plumbers, repair persons, installers, and others. So the millennial generation will be further split, though those who are working 24/7 from their own homes will have a different set of issues to contend with.

It all may require pauses in careers.

Let's hope that by then Shifra at least has pockets.

CHAPTER 7

POCKETS OF SPACE

Lil Beldengreen has recently cleared her mother's attic of the residue and detritus of a few generations, and she feels well qualified to state that we accumulate way too much *stuff*.

Lately a lot of the things we accumulate are electronic, and they are designed to become obsolete within a few years, thus requiring us to buy new and find some way of disposing of the old. (Throwing things in the trash is absolutely not the answer, as the earth does not have enough pockets in which to stash our refuse.) And many of the things we have are plastic or plastic derivatives – even our clothing – and along with our electronics we have fewer and fewer disposal options.

Attic full of pockets of things.

Some young persons today feel that all they own should be stashed on their phones – their important papers, their family birthdays, their schedules, the day's news, their personal photo albums, their mail, their bills, their bank account information, the books they are reading, and much more. They feel that they can throw away their *things* – or never acquire them in the first place – and live light.

They tell us that everything is secure, they back their phones up to a cloud. They feel we should trust that cloud as they do. I have trouble doing that, though. It seems to me they are asking that I deposit my spare house key with an unknown and yet unseen neighbor, who must be trustworthy or he wouldn't live in my neighborhood, where he doesn't own a house.

The cloud is running on strangers' computers, and they have keys to our information. In fact, many strangers who do not host the cloud can have keys to our information, more easily than you would think, from our phones, our computers, our home thermostats, our toasters, our garage door openers....

But okay, everything is on our phones now, to some degree. Yet we have not designed a way to securely and safely carry these phones. We need phone pockets! I cannot repeat that enough.

And as long as we are back to discussing pockets, I can't help but think that as a verb, one meaning of "to pocket" is "to steal." If our information is more easily pocketed than our phones, we are heading in the wrong direction.

For well over a decade, folks have been worried about electronic voting machines being unreliable, unrecountable, unauditable. They worry that without paper ballots verified by the voter, the votes can be stolen.

VoteAllegheny's image of stolen votes.
Used with permission.

If everything is now to be electronic, we have come to a pretty pass. When folks say they nowadays only read electronic books, on devices named for implements of flame and burning (Fire? Kindle?), it definitely brings to mind the fire at the ancient Library at Alexandria, which held a huge amount of the world's knowledge at the time.

In today's version, the library is electronic and one person pulls the electrical plug – perhaps even has Alexa do it – and we have burned our library. Maybe you're reading this book on an electronic device right now! Let's hope your batteries hold up until the end.

ENTIRE ACCUMULATED KNOWLEDGE OF HUMANKIND

The Library of Alexa – as in Alexandria – could easily disappear.

Meanwhile, as long as there are individuals who insist on carrying everything on their phones, which can cost as much as three weeks' take-home pay, I think we should be giving them ample secure pockets in which to carry them. Again, the pockets must be away from the body core while easy to reach, and they must be built into all types of clothing, for all occasions. And they must be secure from pickpockets!

CHAPTER 8

FUTURE POCKETS

There are so many places we need pockets. Even a bride needs a pocket – if not for a phone, then certainly for a hanky!

Maybe we should teach a course in Pockets, or even start a major in Pocketology – with a side of Practical Pocketing. This is meant to be a science course, albeit a soft science, not relegated to an art department. (Please know that we do not disparage art majors – as a Theatre Arts major, the author sewed plenty of pockets into costumes to hold props.)

Degree In Pockets.

There is a lot of hard science involved in pockets, from geometry and calculus (design and maximization) to physics and chemistry (how much can it hold and what should it be made of), and of course biology becomes a huge factor. Still, with all the psychology and sociology and economics involved, we can deem this science soft.

The origin of the word "pocket" is "poke," which is a bag: a pocket is a small bag. (Pocketologists, please don't take that as a reason to build them smaller!) The word "poket" already existed in Middle English, though back in those days the poket generally hung from a tie. I posit that mostly jerkins and leggings for men had them, more than gowns or kirtles for women. There were eventually slits – "fitchets" – cut in the outer garments so that the (male) wearer could reach through to the pouch underneath. Technically, I suppose a codpiece was also a sort of pocket, for carrying the family jewels.

Eventually, those slits became a fashion statement, and there were slashes all over garments. (Think of Walt Disney's Snow White and her sleeves.)

As an aside, the evolution of fashion trends is fascinating. (If only we could learn from it how to evolve pockets faster!) Back in the 1300s folks wore hoods (capuchons) with long, long tails, called liripipes. (Actually, either the hood itself or just the tail could be referred to as a liripipe. We still have them today on academic hoods at graduations.) As the years passed, the fashionable liripipe got longer and longer.

By the 1400s the tails got so long that folks' heads bent forward to counter-balance, and they had to slouch to keep their heads high enough to see where they were going. (Also, the pregnant look was big for women, who took to slouching, too, so everyone was slouching around in what was called the Gothic Slouch.) At some point, someone decided to take off the hood, turn it 90 degrees, and place the part that went around the face over his head. Then he wrapped the tail around and around, leaving the neck part hanging on one side, compacting the capuchon into what would be called a chaperon.

While all this headgear styling was going on, by around the 1500s the slashing had come into vogue. And though the references are sketchy, it seems to have all begun with a need to get to the pockets.

From liripipe to chaperon.

Think what one could store in that liripipe! But we speak of *bygone* pockets.

Where does this trajectory lead us? Well, women of the world, I think we are ready and willing to stand up, letting our things fall from our miniscule pockets, and say, "This far and no farther!" We want our pockets now.

CHAPTER 9

ADDITIONAL POCKETS

In the first chapter of *Babbit*, author Sinclair Lewis described everything that Babbit has in his pockets. It was the author's way of circumscribing the fellow's character. Alas, I would not want to be defined by the tiny items I shove into my tiny pockets.

Many items have been referred to as "pocket" items if they are smaller than usual – a pocket dictionary, a pocket home rototiller, even a pocket battleship.

In fact, our friend Denis lives on and enjoys what is commonly called a "pocket farm," meaning that it is compact!

Pocket farms, though very old, are apparently becoming a hot new model. In Norway, for instance, in the town of Nes, near Oslo, folks are encouraged to buy land and share a communal farm with neighbors.

So even if "pocket" means small when speaking of a farm, it is also the new big thing.

We use the term "pocket" in so many ways.

We have seen far too many bills die by pocket veto, at all levels of government. That is when someone sits on the bill until it is too late to sign it, or until it becomes moot. (I guess this is referring to a *back* pocket, if someone is sitting on it.)

Of course, most of us have played pocket billiards at some point. The angle of incidence equals the angle of reflection!

How about car pockets? Thank goodness they began making most cars with cup holders, though many are not yet big enough or adjustable enough. But how about glove compartments? Where have they gone? If a car has a glove compartment nowadays, it is barely big enough to hold the car's manual.

Lil Beldengreen declares that as long as we are going to suffer climate change, she needs a place in her car beside her seat to stash her wet umbrella after it gets her dryly into the car. We could build a pocket along the door jamb. Or we could build a pocket above the back door, in the ceiling, into which we could insert a wet umbrella after we close the door but before we drag the dripping umbrella across our lap to place on the passenger seat.

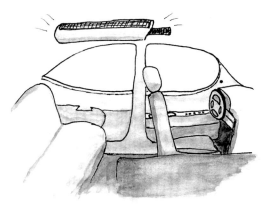

A Pocket for an umbrella.

So let's begin our efforts with clothing pockets. It all comes back to clothing pockets.

Here is an item from the past, by Col. John Alexander Joyce in *Jewels of Memory* (Floriut 1885, second edition published by Gibson Bros., 1896):

"There's No Pocket in a Shroud"
[On the death of a millionaire.]

You must leave your many millions
    And the gay and festive crowd;
Though you roll in royal billions,
    There's no pocket in a shroud.

Whether pauper, prince, or peasant;
    Whether rich or poor or proud –
Remember that there isn't
    Any pocket in a shroud.

You'll have all this world of glory
    With a record long and loud,
And a name in song and story,
    But no pocket in your shroud.

So be gen'rous with your riches,
    Neither vain, nor cold, nor proud,
And you'll gain the golden niches
    In a clime without a cloud!

LIFE OR DEATH

POCKETS OF DANGER

On October 27, 2018, which would have been my late brother Scott's 56th birthday, shots rang out in the hallway of our praying space.

The first sound we heard was a clatter of metal. On later recollection, we each thought it was a coat rack being pulled down upon someone. We kept praying as a few individuals went to help.

Seconds later, we heard an unmistakable automatic weapon resounding through the hallway, the shooter mowing down our friends and colleagues.

One friend, David Rosenthal, had been standing on my right, Rabbi Jeffrey Myers on my left, all three of us leading the Sabbath service. When the shots rang out, David and I fled through a door on the pulpit of the chapel. The rabbi told everyone to get down, and came with us through the door.

The rest of the story has been described in great detail, and likely will come out in the trial of the murderer.

The first words out of my mouth, as we escaped behind a door, were "my cellphone is on the bench." In fact, I had worn clothing that day to remind me of my brother, and the pockets were only 1.5" deep, not sufficient to hold a cellphone. I usually carry a phone on me for just such an emergency, for some amount of security. But this day it was stashed in my new purse – I'd bought a larger purse to hold the new second set of eyeglasses I now need – along with my keys and identification and everything else the men were carrying in their pockets.

Thank goodness men had large pockets! As my friend Joe came through the door with us, our rabbi was already on the phone with 911. A congregant was screaming that her husband had been shot, and I used Joe's phone to call 911 to report the injury and location of the person. I later used Joe's phone to contact my son when we were hiding, as Joe had one of my son's numbers in his phone. Joe and I hid and then escaped together.

During the long period of time while the first responders were cornering the shooter, those who had their phones could call home, alert their colleagues that they were safe, report the incident on social media, etc.

After the shooter had been apprehended and after we each had been interviewed by the FBI, the men who had their keys and ID in their pockets simply handed over their keys and had their cars brought to them by agents from the parking lot of the "crime scene" which was our synagogue. Since my possessions were all still inside the crime scene, I could not have any of it returned for a few days – until they had cleared that part of the room for investigation.

Thus I could not alert worried friends, colleagues, and others that I was still alive. I had my sons contact the few relatives they could, but they had no contacts for my friends. Since no one was notified as to who had been murdered until almost a day later, people were on tenterhooks all that evening, when we were at the regrouping site.

Needless to say, not having large, sufficient pockets was a matter of life and death.

This book had already been in the works when the horror occurred. But the crime has served to punctuate the incredible seriousness of the need for pockets.

We need pockets in our clothing right now – of sufficient strength and size to hold our phones, keys, and wallets if we wish, safely and securely. We should not *need* to carry purses, though I do not advocate abolishing them. We should have pockets on the sides of our legs for our phones. And we should have the ability to carry all sorts of personal items at various locations on our bodies, just as men can do.

The time is long past, we want pockets now.

After the shooting, one of my sons was very solicitous – he offered me chocolate, generously and frequently, to help heal my soul.

While it is obvious that we must stop teaching people to hate, that doesn't really define a positive action. We need a positive action to encourage folks to take.

So we suggest promoting that idea of chocolate. Even though the two items rarely go together well for long, we must:

Teach chocolate.
And teach pockets, too.

WA